Play Ballads

9 hits old and new · Succès d'hier et d'aujourd'hui

Alts und neue Hits

FOR B♭ CLARINET AND PIANO
CLARINETTE EN SI BÉMOL ET PIANO
KLARINETTE IN B UND KLAVIER

Composed and arranged by

JOHN KEMBER

FABER *ff* MUSIC

All nine of the melodies here make excellent concert pieces and have been cherry-picked to help you, whatever your experience, brush up your tone production, breath control and legato tonguing.

John Kember

Ces neuf mélodies font toutes d'excellentes pièces de concert, choisies avec soin pour vous aider, quelle que soit votre expérience, à revoir votre émission sonore, le contrôle de votre souffle et le coup de langue legato.

John Kember

Sämtliche neun Titel eignen sich hervorragend für das Konzert. Die Stücke wurden sorgfältig daraufhin ausgesucht, Trompetern gleich welcher Vorbildung sinnvolles Übungsmaterial für Ansatz, Atemtechnik und Legatospiel zu bieten.

John Kember

© 2001 by Faber Music Ltd
First published in 2001 by Faber Music Ltd
3 Queen Square London WC1N 3AU
Cover illustration by Lynette Williamson
Music processed by Jackie Leigh
Printed in England by Caligraving Ltd

ISBN 0-571-51999-7

To buy Faber Music publications or to find out about the full range of titles available please contact your local music retailer or Faber Music sales enquiries:

Faber Music Limited, Burnt Mill, Elizabeth Way, Harlow, CM20 2HX England
Tel: +44 (0)1279 82 89 82   Fax: +44 (0)1279 82 89 83
sales@fabermusic.com   www.fabermusic.com

Contents

Killing Me Softly

Charles Fox
and Norman Gimbel
arr. John Kember

Hello

Lionel Richie
arr. John Kember

Something About You

John Kember

Once In A While

John Kember

A Quiet Place

John Kember

Unhurried ♩ = 88

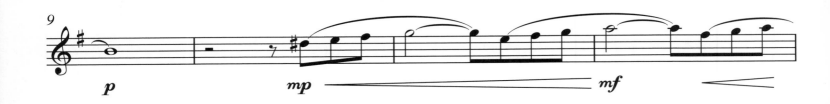

What The World Needs Now

Burt Bacharach
arr. John Kember

In The Hush Of The Night

John Kember

Your Song

Elton John & Bernie Taupin
arr. John Kember

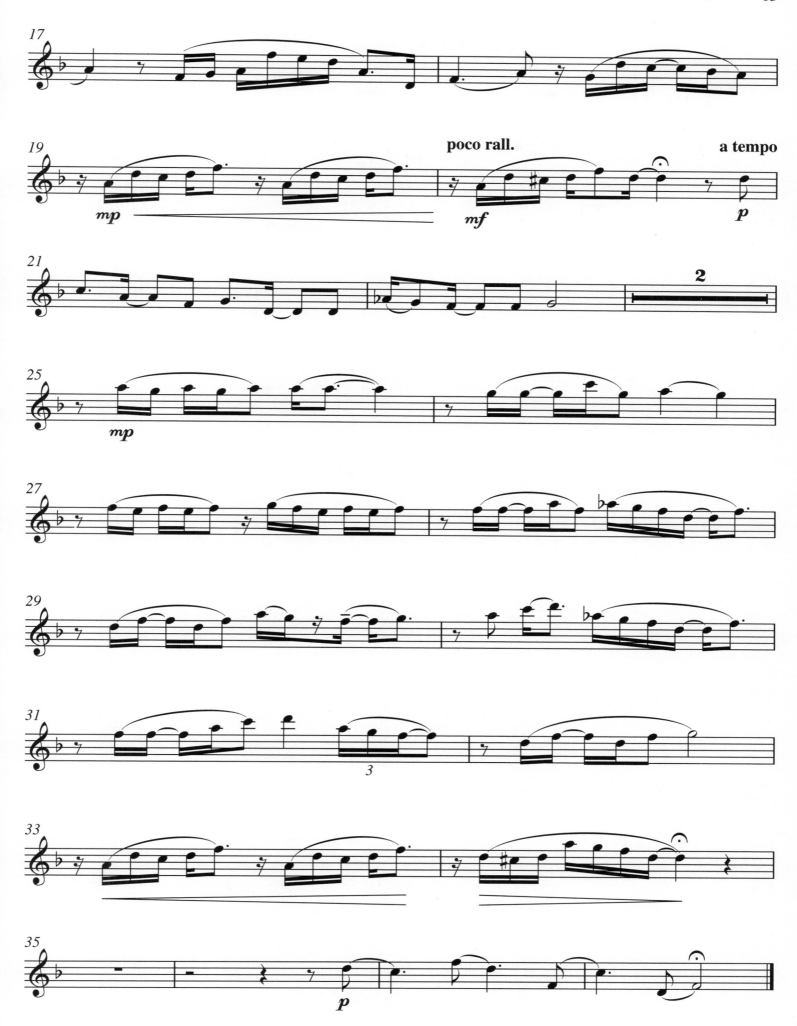

If I Did It All Again

John Kember

Play Ballads

9 hits old and new · Succès d'hier et d'aujourd'hui · Alts und neue Hits

FOR B♭ CLARINET AND PIANO
CLARINETTE EN SI BÉMOL ET PIANO
KLARINETTE IN B UND KLAVIER

Contents

FABER *ff* MUSIC

© 2001 by Faber Music Ltd
First published in 2001 by Faber Music Ltd
3 Queen Square London WC1N 3AU
Cover illustration by Lynette Williamson
Music processed by Jackie Leigh
Printed in England by Caligraving Ltd
All rights reserved

ISBN 0-571-51999-7

To buy Faber Music publications or to find out about the full range of titles available
please contact your local music retailer or Faber Music sales enquiries:

Faber Music Limited, Burnt Mill, Elizabeth Way, Harlow, CM20 2HX England
Tel: +44 (0)1279 82 89 82   Fax: +44 (0)1279 82 89 83
sales@fabermusic.com   www.fabermusic.com

Killing Me Softly

Charles Fox
and Norman Gimbel
arr. John Kember

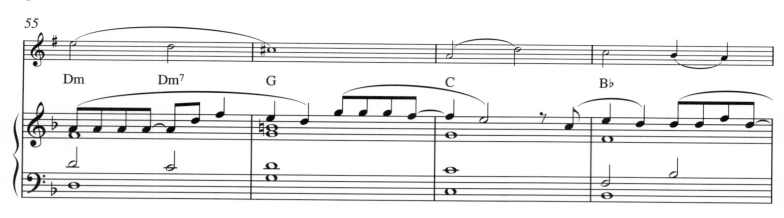

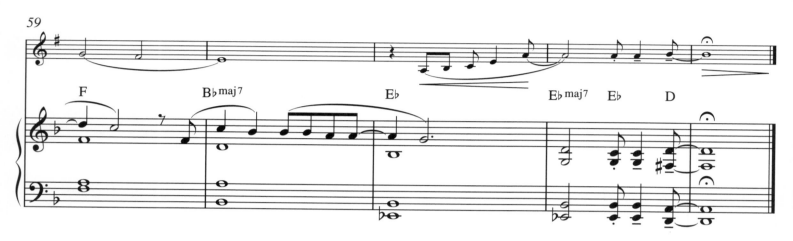

Hello

Lionel Richie
arr. John Kember

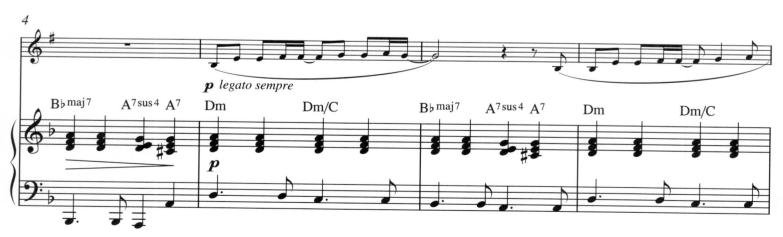

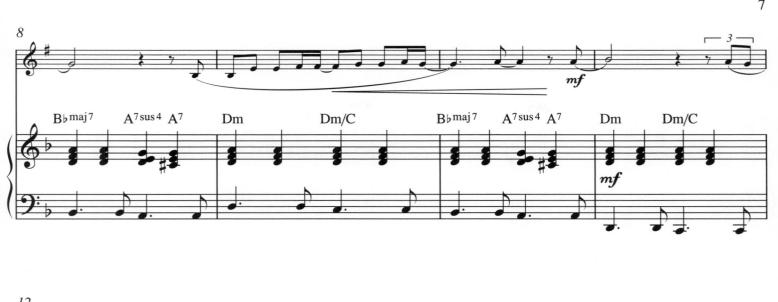

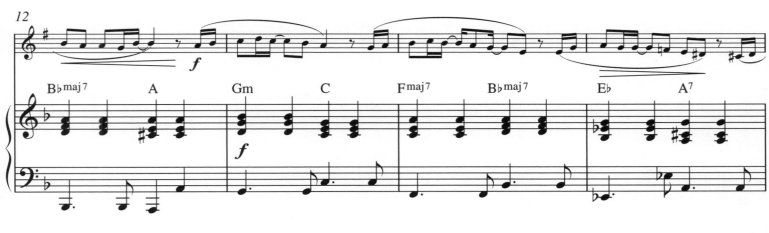

Something About You

John Kember

Once In A While

John Kember

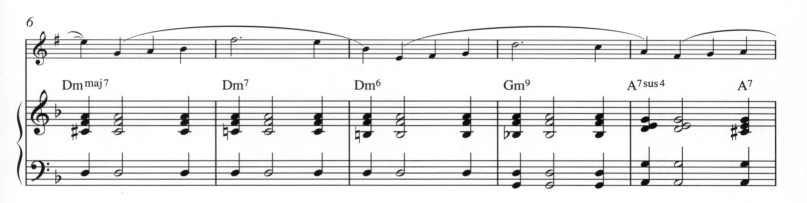

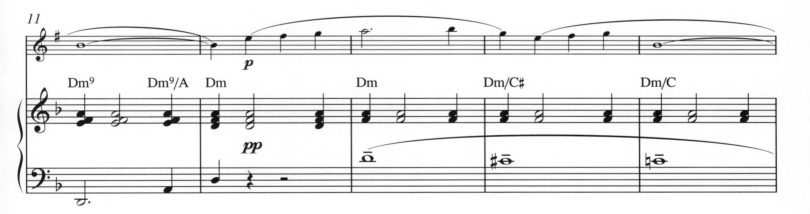

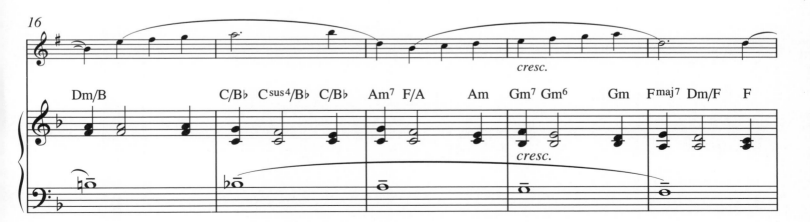

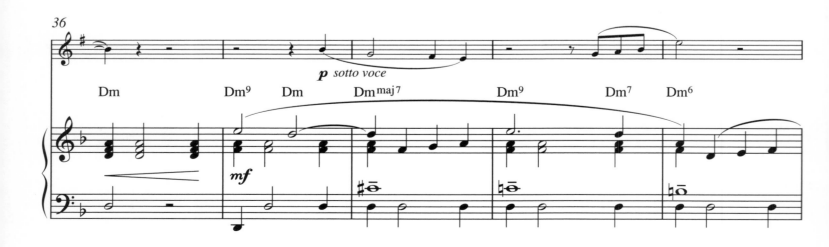

A Quiet Place

John Kember

What The World Needs Now

Burt Bacharach
arr. John Kember

In The Hush Of The Night

John Kember

Your Song

Elton John & Bernie Taupin
arr. John Kember

With a gentle beat ♩ = 48

If I Did It All Again

John Kember